D1326248

330.122

Ideas of the
Modern World

Capitalism

R. G. Grant

HODDER
Wayland

an imprint of Hodder Children's Books

Published in Great Britain in 2001 by Hodder Wayland, an imprint of Hodder Children's Books.

This book was prepared for Hodder Wayland by Ruth Nason.

Series design: Simon Borrough

A catalogue record for this book is available from the British Library.

ISBN 0 7502 2750 8

Printed and bound in Italy by
G. Canale & C. S.p.A., Turin

Hodder Children's Books
A division of Hodder Headline Limited
338 Euston Road, London NW1 3BH

Acknowledgements
The author and publishers thank the following for permission to reproduce photographs: Camera Press: cover, pages 5, 53; Mary Evans Picture Library: pages 6, 10, 12, 13, 14, 15, 16, 17l, 29, 42; Peter Newark's American Pictures: pages 1, 20, 21, 22, 23, 24, 27, 30t, 31, 34, 37, 44; Popperfoto: pages 17r, 19, 25, 28, 30b, 32, 35, 38t, 38b, 40, 41, 43, 46, 48, 51, 52, 54, 55, 57, 58; Still Pictures: pages 4 (Ron Giling), 8-9 (Mark Edwards), 50 (Gil Moti).

Contents

What is Capitalism?

Capitalism is the economic system that dominates the world we live in. Since the late eighteenth century, it has transformed the ways people live and work. It has allowed humans to produce goods and provide services in ever-increasing quantities, creating unprecedented wealth for some. It has also promoted ceaseless technical innovation, from the steam engine to the Internet. And yet capitalism has always been controversial. Its critics have accused it of causing poverty, inequality, social disruption and massive damage to the environment.

The fundamental idea on which capitalism rests is that, if individuals try to make as much money as possible, this will be good for humankind as a whole. People who run successful businesses accumulate capital – that is, assets in the form of money or productive equipment such as machinery. They use this capital to produce more goods or to provide more services, aiming to make the highest profits possible. In order to

Capitalism leads to a society where there is money to spend, and businesses produce and advertise so many things that there is pressure to spend it.

maximize their profits, they constantly seek out new ways of making things more cheaply, or look for new items to manufacture, or pay for new types of machinery to be introduced. In this way, capitalism generates material progress as a by-product of the pursuit of profit.

A silk factory in India. Modern machinery mass-produces goods that were once hand-made by skilled craftspeople.

Selfish but good

In *The Wealth of Nations*, published in 1776, Scottish philosopher Adam Smith argued that people's natural selfishness led them to fulfil society's needs in a free-market system. He wrote:

'It is not from the benevolence of the butcher, the brewer, or the baker, that we expect our dinner, but from their regard to their own interest.'

Capitalism is supposed to lead to the good of everyone through the operation of the 'free market'. If people are free to buy and sell goods for any price they think fit, competition between different producers should ensure that prices are always as low as they possibly can be. The free market is also supposed to encourage the most efficient possible production and distribution of goods and services, because inefficient businesses will go to the wall. It tends to ensure that the goods produced are things that people want, because no business can survive if it produces goods that do not sell.

5

The pre-capitalist world

There is nothing new about people producing and selling goods for profit. This has happened throughout human history and in almost all parts of the world. Merchants have often traded over large areas of the earth. Two thousand years ago, for example, wealthy citizens of Ancient Rome could buy goods brought to Europe from as far afield as China and India. In the thirteenth century Muslim bankers based in Cairo, Egypt, ran thriving trade networks which stretched across the world from China in the east to Italy in the west.

But in the pre-capitalist world, business interests were not dominant in society. Merchants and traders were generally held in low esteem, considered way beneath warriors and landowners. There was a widespread suspicion of making money through business. Religions tended to preach against 'usury' – lending money at interest – and to denounce the pursuit of profit as 'greed'. Where wealth was created, it was

This sixteenth-century drawing shows Arab traders being harassed by bandits as they make their way to trade with a European ship.

Capitalists kept in their place

Japan under the Tokugawa shoguns (1603-1867) is an example of a society in which merchants were wealthy, but at the same time despised and limited in influence. In theory, there was a strict hierarchy in Japanese society. At the top were the warriors, or samurai. Below them were peasants, then craftsmen, and finally, the lowest of the low, the merchants. By the nineteenth century, many Japanese merchants had become rich and many samurai were heavily in debt, owing the merchants large sums of money. But it was still not possible for a capitalist system to emerge in Japan while trade was held in such low esteem and government and law were organized for the benefit of warriors and landowners.

often plundered by unscrupulous rulers or used up in massive public works such as the building of pyramids or cathedrals. Rich individuals spent their money on lavish entertainments, works of art or jewellery, rather than investing it to make yet more money.

Pre-capitalist societies tended to value stability and security, rather than change and growth. They tried to ensure that everyone knew their place in society and stayed in it. Most people were tied to a ruler, land-owner or master by duties of service, or were restricted in the jobs they could take up. Governments or bodies such as guilds often tried rigidly to control wages and prices. In any case, buying and selling played a limited part in life, as many people produced the food they ate and even made their own clothes and tools.

Wealth and hardship

Capitalism tends to create a quite different kind of world. It puts money at the centre of society. It largely replaces relationships of loyalty, tradition or duty with purely financial relationships – such as that between an employer and employee. It favours social mobility, opening up a path of opportunity for ambitious individuals, but also punishing those who fail to adapt to change or take care of themselves.

In one sense, capitalism's success is indisputable. Until the capitalist era, no society ever achieved a sustained, on-going increase in wealth. Human prosperity had only varied within fairly narrow limits. But over the last 200 years, the pursuit of profit in a free market has proved its ability to generate increased wealth – that is, goods and services – with apparently no limit. It has created a world market, so that everyone, from a New Yorker to a villager on a Pacific coral island, participates in the capitalist system.

Unprecedented growth

Economists have tried to put into figures the vast increase in human productive capacity since the start of the capitalist era. In the developed world, mostly North America and Western Europe, average output per head was reckoned to have risen from $180 in 1750 to over $3,000 in the 1980s. In the underdeveloped countries, such as China and India, the rise had been much smaller, but even there output per head had more than doubled – from $180 to over $400. Meanwhile the world population has grown astonishingly, from less than one billion people in 1750 to six billion in 1999.

A major concern is that pursuit of profit leads to environmental damage. This area of the Amazon rainforest has been cleared by prospectors mining tin ore.

For millions of people, however, capitalism has brought insecurity and hardship. Wherever it has arrived, local crafts and traditional ways of life have crumbled, or survived only in part and with difficulty. Forced to sell their labour in the free market, working people have often seen their incomes driven down as capitalists in search of profit try to reduce their wage bills. Some have had to work for excessively long hours in unhealthy conditions. For others, unemployment has brought poverty as businesses offload workers whenever they are not needed.

Wealth and poverty

Capitalism has always tended to create inequality. In 1999 it was estimated that Bill Gates, the founder of the Microsoft corporation and the world's richest man, was worth more than $100 billion. At the other end of the capitalist system, about half the world's population, some 3 billion people, were reckoned to be living off less than $2 each per day.

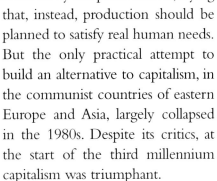

Meanwhile, in the modern capitalist world, business people such as Bill Gates or Rupert Murdoch command corporations with budgets larger than those of many national governments. Their personal wealth is counted in billions of dollars and they exercise much more power than most presidents or prime ministers. The decisions they take, with a view to profit, can alter the lives of millions of people.

Capitalism triumphant

To some people, capitalism has always seemed plain wrong. Critics have attacked it for encouraging selfish individualism at the expense of the community, and for putting material wealth above spiritual values. They have denounced a world driven by the profit motive, saying that, instead, production should be planned to satisfy real human needs. But the only practical attempt to build an alternative to capitalism, in the communist countries of eastern Europe and Asia, largely collapsed in the 1980s. Despite its critics, at the start of the third millennium capitalism was triumphant.

This book will describe the rise of capitalism in Europe in the eighteenth century, how it came to dominate the world in the nineteenth, and how it survived many upsets in the twentieth century to create today's 'global economy'. It will also look at the problems associated with the success of capitalism, and ask whether these problems can be solved.

The Rise of Industrial Capitalism

The origins of the modern capitalist system lie in an upsurge of business activity and technical innovation in Northwestern Europe in the eighteenth century. In one country, Britain, this process first took off into self-sustained economic growth with the start of what is often called the 'industrial revolution'.

Trade and innovation

New attitudes had begun to make themselves felt in Western Europe from the mid-seventeenth century. In the Netherlands, Britain and France, merchants achieved a new status, and trade was recognized as crucial to national wealth and power. Governments

The Amsterdam stock exchange (shown in a painting of c. 1668) was built in 1608-11. People came there to buy and sell shares in commercial enterprises.

Mercantalism

Between roughly 1650 and 1750, the dominant economic theory in Europe was 'mercantilism'. European governments believed that, in order to become wealthy, their countries must export more than they imported. The result would be a steady accumulation of gold or silver money in the country. Colonies were expected to trade exclusively with the mother country. Much business was in the form of monopolies granted by the government – for example, the British East India Company was given the sole right to trade with India.

actively encouraged manufacture and commerce. A spirit of rational enquiry developed, which favoured practical innovation and the search for improvements in all areas of life. In Britain and the Netherlands, elected parliaments set limits to the power of the monarch, creating a climate of law and security which encouraged business. Increasingly, people sought to improve their fortunes through hard work, saving and investment. Even the landowning aristocracy, who had traditionally despised trade, began to adopt a business-like attitude to exploiting the economic potential of their land.

By the second half of the eighteenth century, the rising prosperity of Britain, in particular, was attracting international attention. British agriculture was the most 'modern' in Europe. Land-owners were systematically increasing output from their land by exploring new techniques and new crops. The rural population were mostly wage labourers. Many poverty-stricken rural workers moved to Britain's swelling towns and cities, providing a pool of labour for new enterprises. Rising agricultural production made it possible to feed this growing urban

The Protestant work ethic

In 1904 German sociologist Max Weber suggested that the 'Protestant ethic' was partly responsible for the success of capitalism in Europe. He said that Protestants believed that hard work was good and leisure (or 'idleness') was bad. They also favoured saving and investing money, rather than spending it on luxuries. According to Weber, these attitudes made Protestant countries such as the Netherlands and Britain most suitable for the growth of capitalism.

population. Britain had an expanding national market for goods, and its shipping provided access to overseas markets as well. Traders had already become rich carrying slaves from Africa to plantations in Britain's colonies, and bringing plantation products – such as sugar, coffee and tea – back to Britain.

Industrial revolution

The economic take-off of the industrial revolution is reckoned to have started around 1780. British entrepreneurs, often with only a small amount of capital to start with, began to mass-produce cotton goods. They set up factories, known as cotton mills, where the process of spinning cotton was rationalized to achieve maximum output. To keep wages low, they employed mostly women and children, and they applied quite simple inventions such as the spinning jenny and Arkwright's mule, plus James Watt's steam engine as a source of power. Cotton goods were soon being produced so quickly and cheaply that they flooded the home market and conquered worldwide markets as well.

Women workers at a cotton mill in 1851.

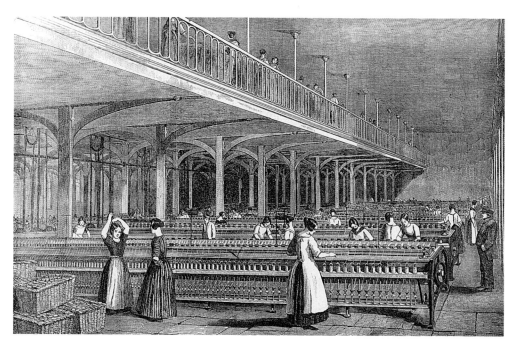

Adam Smith (1723-90)

Born in Scotland, Dr Adam Smith was a philosopher who became interested in how the economy could be organized to create a better, more prosperous society. In 1776 he published *An Inquiry into the Nature and Causes of the Wealth of Nations,* which gives the first description of what we would now call free-market capitalism.

Smith argued that the 'hidden hand' of the market would naturally tend to make the economy as efficient – and therefore the country as wealthy – as possible. Prices would fall to the lowest possible level, benefiting everyone as consumers. A 'division of labour' would develop, with individuals and countries specializing in tasks they were best at. And competition would drive business people to introduce ingenious new machines, in order to increase productivity.

The job of the government was to defend the country, uphold the law – above all protecting property – and build what is now called infrastructure (roads, bridges, canals, and so on) to make economic activity possible. Apart from that, it should simply free business of all regulations and controls, intervening only to stop anything interfering with the operation of the free market.

Smith's book was immensely influential in its time, and has remained so to this day.

Statistics tell the story of Britain's unprecedented economic growth. The output of cotton cloth from Britain rose from 40 million yards in 1785 to more than 2,000 million yards in 1850 – by which time Britain was making more than half the cotton goods produced in the entire world. British coalmines, iron foundries and potteries also flourished, creating immense fortunes for their owners. By 1850 Britain was producing almost 70 per cent of the world's coal and 50 per cent of its pig iron.

Stock market madness

Early in the rise of capitalism, one of its most characteristic institutions developed: the stock market. This was a mechanism allowing people with spare money a chance to buy a share in capitalist enterprises. They bought a 'share' in a business, which gave them the right to part of the profits. These shares were bought and sold on the stock market. However, share trading soon showed a tendency to generate wild speculation, with shares often changing hands for prices that had no relation to the real value of the

business. For example, on the London Stock Exchange in 1720, investors flocked to buy shares in the South Sea Company, a well-publicized business that was, in fact, worthless. Because people were so keen to buy the shares, their price went up. And seeing the price rise, people became even more eager to buy, paying ever larger sums of money for the shares, confident that they would be able to sell them for even more money later. Eventually, though, the worthlessness of the company was revealed and the 'South Sea Bubble' burst. Thousands of people lost their money as the shares they had bought became so much scrap paper.

Above: This London street scene shows the enthusiasm with which people tried to buy shares in the South Sea Company in 1720.

Gold from the slums

The speed with which wealth grew in Britain astonished observers at the time, who quickly recognized that something quite new was happening in the world. They were fascinated and appalled by the contrast between the immense fortunes being made by the 'captains of industry' and the atrocious conditions endured by the industrial workers. Visiting Manchester, one of the new industrial towns, in 1830, Frenchman Alexis de Tocqueville commented: 'From this filthy sewer pure gold flows.'

Karl Marx in his study in London. He saw capitalism as one stage of human development, which would eventually be overthrown. (See page 27.)

Factory work

Writing in the 1850s, one of capitalism's most famous critics, the revolutionary philosopher Karl Marx, denounced the impact of the capitalist system on workers who had previously practised a craft, but were forced into factory work. He said the system would

'mutilate the labourer into a fragment of a man, degrade him to the level of appendage of a machine, destroy every remnant of charm in his work and turn it into hated toil ...'

Although many working people were attracted to the factories by the prospect of an escape from the backwardness and poverty of rural life, there is no doubt that the new industrial capitalism imposed a harsh, even brutal regime on its workers. Never before had such discipline been required of them. Under close supervision, they were forced to repeat mechanical tasks for 12 hours or more a day, at the rhythm of the machine. Their reward was to be able to afford to live in a polluted slum. Life expectancy in some of the new industrial towns was half that in the countryside around them.

Slums and money

Friedrich Engels, a friend and colleague of Karl Marx, described walking through the industrial town of Manchester with a middle-class Englishman in the early 1840s:

'I spoke to him about the disgraceful unhealthy slums and ... the disgusting condition of that part of town in which the factory workers lived ... He listened patiently and [then] remarked: "And yet there is a great deal of money made here."'

★ Catching up

Historians have long debated why the industrial revolution happened in Europe, rather than, for example, in China or India. In the eighteenth century, India led the world in the production of cotton goods for export, and China had a sophisticated economy whose manufactures included porcelain and silks much sought after by Europeans. One argument is that, in both India and China, state control was excessive and the spirit of enterprise and innovation was discouraged. Another argument is that the Europeans created their industrial revolution because, being more backward than Asia, they needed to catch up.

Even worse hit were those who lost their traditional jobs because of competition from the factories. For example, when weaving, the second stage of cotton-goods manufacture, began to be industrialized through the introduction of power looms around 1810, weavers who worked on hand-looms in country villages saw their livelihood ruined. Some became 'Luddites', breaking up the new machinery in a vain effort to preserve their craft jobs.

The rise of liberalism

Much of Britain's new-found wealth flowed into the pockets of people who were of quite lowly social origins, although some of the traditional landed aristocracy were also enriched – they, for example, owned most of the coalmines. The new moneyed class of factory owners and entrepreneurs quickly became a political force, generally identified with 'liberalism'. The liberals opposed the privileges of the aristocracy and the powers of the monarchy, arguing for a 'modern' society in which every individual was equal before the law. They advocated total free trade – the

In 1811-12, groups of hand-loom weavers destroyed new machinery in textile factories, which they feared would put them out of work. They became known as 'Luddites', after one machine-breaker, Ned Ludd. Today the word is used for anyone who resists technological innovation.

ending of all tariffs on imports or exports – and the sweeping away of any rules and regulations that might block the operation of the free market.

British governments were increasingly responsive to these arguments. They used the full force of the law against any people who tried to resist the onward march of capitalism and industry. Laws were passed making it illegal for workers to 'combine' – that is, form what we would call a trade union – to seek higher wages or better conditions. Such action by workers was condemned as being against the principles of the free market. Machine-breaking could be punished by hanging. Financial support for the poor, provided according to the traditional precepts of Christian charity, was taken away, on the grounds that it would make people reluctant to work and so would

Malthus and Ricardo

British economists of the early nineteenth century were deeply pessimistic about the possibility of any increase in the general standard of living, however successful business might be. In his *Essay on the Principle of Population* (1807), Thomas Malthus argued that increasing wealth would only encourage people to have more children. The population would grow until the wealth was used up and the majority once more lived in abject poverty and near starvation.

Influenced by Malthus, David Ricardo argued in his book, *Principles of Political Economy* (1817), that the 'inevitable' tendency of a free market was to keep workers' wages at subsistence level – that is, just high enough for them and their families to survive. According to Ricardo, industry could generate great wealth, but this prosperity could never belong to the majority of the population.

push up wages. The triumph of free trade was almost complete in 1846, when the Corn Laws, import tariffs designed to protect British landowners from the competition of cheap foreign wheat, were abolished.

Acting against abuses

While the free-market principles were sometimes systematically applied in Britain, there was also a revulsion against the abuses of the new factory system. In 1833, a Factory Act appointed factory inspectors to check on the employment conditions of women and children, and in 1847 a ten-hour working day for women and older children was decreed. It was an early example of the simple fact that the harsh principles of capitalism would never be applied with their full logic.

Capitalism and slavery

More than six million slaves were carried across the Atlantic from Africa to the West Indies and North and South America in the eighteenth century. Large profits were made from this trade, and from the plantations worked by slaves in the New World. The rapid accumulation of wealth through the slave trade and the exploitation of slave labour, especially by British merchants and plantation owners, almost certainly contributed to the economic take-off of the industrial revolution. This provided a large supply of surplus money that could be invested in Britain. But capitalist industry in the end preferred a mobile labour force of free workers. Therefore factory owners were among the leaders of movements to abolish the slave trade and slavery, and these movements had largely succeeded by the 1870s.

The industrial revolution moved into a new phase when the railways began to be built in the 1830s. Railways needed iron and steel and coal in massive quantities. As they spread, they stimulated a huge new wave of investment in heavy industry. By 1850 industrial capitalism was solidly established in Britain and was at last gathering speed in other areas of Europe, especially Belgium, France and parts of Germany, and in the USA. It was evident that the world had set off in a new direction that would not be reversed.

Capitalism's 'Golden Age'

From 1850 to 1914, for many Europeans and North Americans, capitalism seemed synonymous with civilization and progress. Rapid economic growth continued and spread. Steamships and the telegraph linked the capitalist heartlands – Western Europe and the USA – to all parts of the globe. International trade flourished as raw materials and foodstuffs flowed into the industrialized areas from around the world, and a tide of manufactured goods, capital and labour flowed in the opposite direction.

The quay in Sidney, Australia, c. 1883, a time when steamships were beginning to replace sail.

The gold standard

Up to 1914, the fixed value of different national currencies was maintained by the 'gold standard'. Each country's unit of currency – for example, the US dollar – was agreed to be worth a precise quantity of gold. The country had to hold enough gold reserves to back up the currency, so that, if holders of dollar bills, for example, had tried to exchange them for gold, they could have been paid in full. It gave people great confidence in the long-term value of their currency.

Scenes at the Carnegie iron works, in Pittsburgh, Pennsylvania, from the front cover of a weekly journal, 'Scientific American', March 1880.

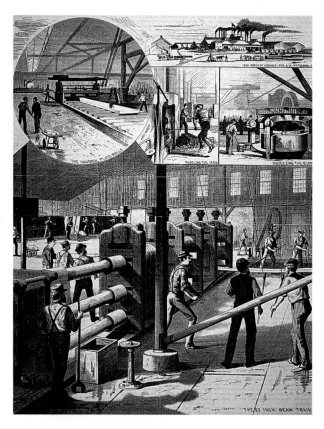
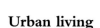

Britain lost its lead in manufacturing as the USA and Germany grew into industrial giants, but the City of London remained the world's financial hub. Trade benefited from a system of stable exchange rates between different countries across the world. For example, one British pound could always be exchanged for exactly the same number of US dollars, year in year out. The same was true for German Marks and French francs. This meant that exporters and importers operated in secure and predicatable conditions.

Urban living

Cities such as London, Berlin, Paris, New York and Chicago grew at an unprecedented rate. Around 1850, Britain became the first country in world history to have the majority of its population in towns and cities rather than working on the land; by 1900, less than one in ten British people lived in the country. Although all the world's cities were disfigured by poverty and slums, they were progressively better lit, equipped with proper sanitation, and effectively policed. Museums, symphony orchestras and opera houses, often funded directly by capitalist millionaires, reflected a new civic pride. Universal education created widespread literacy.

A cartoon of Andrew Carnegie holding four of the many libraries that he endowed.

Andrew Carnegie (1835-1919)

Some of the new millionaires of business and finance felt guilty about making so much money out of the work of poorly paid labourers. They attempted to appease their consciences by becoming public benefactors, providing model housing for workers or funding museums and other charitable foundations. Andrew Carnegie was the most striking of the millionaire 'philanthropists'. He was born into a poor family in Scotland. When he was 13, his family emigrated to Pittsburgh in the USA. Carnegie worked as a railway clerk and a telegraph operator, before eventually investing his savings in what grew to be the largest iron and steel manufacturer in the USA. Despite his vast fortune, he expressed a contempt for money except as a path to higher spiritual values. He declared that it was 'the noblest possible use of wealth' to bring 'sweetness and light' to the toiling masses. Carnegie had given over $350 million to charity by the time of his death in 1919.

In politics, there was general agreement on the need for elected parliaments, whether in republics, such as France and the USA, or in monarchies, such as Britain or Germany. In Europe, the ruling class was a mix of the new 'bourgeoisie' – industrialists, bankers and entrepreneurs – and the old landed ruling class, which adjusted to the new conditions. Governments mostly treated their citizens as equal before the law and respected civil liberties.

The long reach of capitalism

The world market meant that changes in an industrialized country could profoundly affect the lives of people across the world. For example, the growth of the British cotton industry in the first half of the nineteenth century caused a huge expansion of slavery in the southern USA, since black slaves on plantations produced most of the raw cotton that Britain needed. The export of cheap British cotton goods in turn destroyed the livelihood of workers in the cotton industry in India.

The growth of the capitalist economies also affected animals. For instance, sharply rising demand for ivory, needed for the manufacture of billiard balls and pianos, led to the massacre of elephants in Africa. Vast numbers of whales were killed for a whole range of products that they could contribute to expanding capitalism.

Imperial developments

The industrialized states took direct control of much of the globe, creating empires, and indirectly controlled the rest through the power of their industry and finance. Moneyed Europeans invested in railway construction, ports, canals and mines, in locations from Peru to Siberia and from South Africa to China. Vast areas of the world were occupied by European settlers – notably the American West, Argentina, Australia and New Zealand. Resistance was swept aside by the military power of weapons mass-produced by the new industries. Countries such as India and China, which as recently as 1800 had been major net exporters of goods to Europe, became mere markets for industrial goods from the developed world and sites for

Swedish settlers in Nebraska, in the American West, c. 1895.

profitable investment. Japan was the only non–white state to manage the transformation into an industrial power by 1914.

As capitalism grew, it changed. This was partly a result of the different situations and traditions of different countries. In the USA, the leading money-makers of the mid-nineteenth century were known as the 'robber barons', because of their unscrupulousness in the pursuit of profit. Fraud and violence were normal in the totally unregulated, rapidly expanding American economy. In continental Europe, by contrast, governments played a far more active role in promoting industrial growth than had been the case in Britain. So did large banks and finance houses.

Price fixing and protection

As the scale of capitalist organizations increased, Adam Smith's idea of competition in a free market began to seem out of date. A single industrial giant tended to control a whole sector of a national economy, or a number of large companies joined together in a 'cartel' or 'trust' to fix prices. In the USA, from 1890, anti-trust acts were passed in an effort to prevent price-rigging and ensure fair competition, but they had only limited success. Capitalist businesses increasingly controlled the market.

This cartoon from 1889 expresses the idea that American politicians were controlled by the giant trusts.

A pure free market also failed to operate internationally. Britain could not make the rest of the world accept its own view of the virtue of

Britain, France, Russia and the USA all wanted to break Japan's policy of isolation to start trading there. In 1854, Japan gave in and signed a treaty with the USA, after Commodore Matthew Perry had arrived with a naval force.

free trade. Most industrial countries, including the USA, practised protectionism, erecting import duties to keep out foreign products which competed with their own industries or agriculture. The industrial countries refused to allow the rest of the world to protect itself against free trade, however. Military power was used against both China and Japan to force them to let in European and North American goods.

Friedrich List (1789-1846)

Born in the German state of Württemberg, List emigrated to the USA in the 1820s, then returned to Europe as a US consul. In his book *National System of Political Economy* (1841), he argued that a strong government could be the motor driving industrial capitalism. Rejecting Adam Smith's idea of free trade, List said that governments should use import duties to protect their industries from foreign competition. He also believed that the state should actively encourage economic growth through heavy investment in roads and railways, and through providing a high standard of education. List's idea of state-backed capitalism was very influential in continental Europe, and especially in Germany – it is sometimes referred to as 'Prussian capitalism'.

★ Social Darwinism

English philosopher Herbert Spencer (1820-1903) justified the triumph of capitalism and European imperialism by reference to Charles Darwin's theory of evolution through natural selection. Spencer's theory, known as Social Darwinism, applied the principle of the 'survival of the fittest' to society. He argued that people who made lots of money had proved themselves the fitter in the harsh but healthy world of free competition. Any attempt to lessen the effect of competition would only allow weaklings to survive, harming the quality of the human race. This theory was especially popular in the USA around the start of the twentieth century.

" God's law of business

American millionaire owner of Standard Oil, John D. Rockefeller (1839-1937) justified his wealth as the result of natural selection:

'The growth of a large business is merely the survival of the fittest ... It is merely the working out of a law of nature and a law of God.'

Products for the masses

Capitalism's ability to generate technological innovation and discover new markets was unflagging. Companies set up research departments to apply science systematically to new products. Electricity, oil and chemicals opened up new potential as old industries based on coal and iron stagnated. The USA proved especially skilled at the mass-production of machines, starting with rifles and sewing machines, and moving on to automobiles with the Model T Ford around 1910. The first production lines were

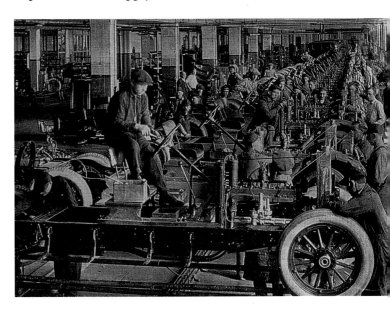

The final assembly line at the Ford factory, c. 1927.

introduced, making factories even more efficient. The power of advertising grew, targeting a mass public in the expanding cities. In the early twentieth century, the cinema and newspapers began to create a new popular culture marketed for profit. These developments suggested that capitalism might progress by making its workers better off, so that they could consume the products of industry – rather than just exploiting them at the lowest possible wage.

Boom and slump

Although capitalism was full of confidence and assurance, reflected in its palatial banks and stock markets, it still had its problems. The age-old pattern of good and bad harvests, which had brought periodic hardship to pre-industrial societies, was replaced by the capitalist cycle of boom and slump. Economists had recognized this as a fact of life by 1870. Slumps tended to occur periodically because of over-production saturating the market. This led to a wave of business failures and factory closures. The working population had little defence against the impact of slumps, which struck in the 1840s, 1870s and 1890s, bringing hardship and unemployment.

"Against struggle

In the mid-nineteenth century, British thinker John Stuart Mill expressed his doubts about the new competitive world of capitalism:

'I am not charmed with the ideal of life held out by those who think that the normal state of human beings is struggling to get on; that the trampling, crushing, elbowing, and treading on each other's heels, which form the existing type of social life, are the most desirable lot of human beings.'

In Europe in the late nineteenth and early twentieth centuries, state-backed unemployment insurance and pensions began to lessen the harshness of a worker's life under capitalism. Trade unions were also allowed to develop, first among skilled workers, but later among the mass of dockers and transport workers. Some skilled workers became distinctly better off, benefiting from rising wages and low prices. But there was still plenty of abject poverty – New York, for example, was notorious for the poor living conditions of many of its inhabitants.

Karl Marx (1818-83)

Born in Trier, Germany, Karl Marx lived most of his life in exile in London, where he worked tirelessly for the overthrow of capitalism. In his book *Das Kapital*, the first volume of which was published in 1867, he argued that capitalism exploited and impoverished the majority of workers by stealing the wealth they created. This wealth went to enrich a minority of capitalists and the

bourgeoisie (middle classes). Marx accepted that capitalism was a necessary stage in human development, because it vastly increased the amount of goods that could be produced. But he argued that the industrial working class created by capitalism would eventually overthrow the system. The workers would take the products of industry for themselves, ending poverty and exploitation.

An American cartoon of 1880 echoes Marx's point that capitalists 'grow fat' on the backs of workers.

Slaves of the machine

Irish author Oscar Wilde, an advocate of socialism in the 1890s, argued that the capitalist system stopped machinery being used to make people happy and free:

'Up to the present, man has been, to a certain extent, the slave of machinery ... This, however, is the result of our property system and our system of competition. One man owns a machine that does the work of 500 men. Five hundred men are, as a consequence, thrown out of employment ... At present machinery competes against man. Under proper conditions machinery will serve man.'

Socialist opposition

By the early twentieth century, organized opposition to capitalism was widespread in the industrialized countries. Mass socialist parties campaigned for the productive power of the machine age to be used for the benefit of the majority of workers, rather than a wealthy minority of owners. Trade unionists clashed with employers in large-scale strikes, both sides sometimes resorting to violence. It is doubtful whether these socialist movements could in themselves have mounted a serious threat to the reign of capital, had the capitalist powers not plunged into a suicidal war. The conflict that broke out in Europe in 1914 shook the world economic system to its roots and ended capitalism's 'golden age'.

Capitalism in Crisis

The period from 1914 to 1945 was a time of global war, economic depression and communist revolution. Faith in capitalism was severely shaken by these experiences. By the end of the period, few people believed that the capitalist system would simply deliver the goods if governments left it alone.

War economy

In 1914, full-scale war broke out in Europe, the heartland of world capitalism. From 1917, the USA also took part in what became known as the First World War. In an effort to concentrate national resources towards the one overriding goal of winning the war, the combatant countries instituted state control of the economy to a degree completely at odds with free-market capitalism. Governments controlled prices and wages, rationed food supplies and other necessities, told businesses what to produce, directed investment and allotted workers to industries.

Women workers at the Krupp arms factory in Essen, Germany, during the First World War. The war used the immense productive power of capitalist industry for the purpose of mass destruction.

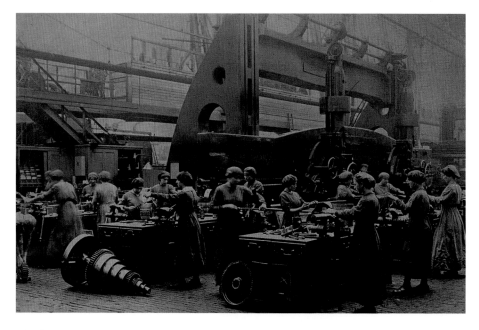

The extent of state control varied from country to country – Germany's control of the economy in the First World War became so extreme that it was described as 'war socialism'. But even in the USA, where there was most resistance to the idea of government interference, federal control of the economy was considerable. The experience of government intervention in the economy during wartime changed people's ideas of what the state could do.

In search of normalcy

Nonetheless, at the end of the war, governments were eager to return to the old world of virtually unregulated capitalism – referred to in the USA as 'normalcy'. Unfortunately, the system of world trade and finance that had existed for the previous century was totally disrupted. The war had cost vast sums of money. Britain emerged from the conflict massively in debt to the USA, which was by now the world's strongest economy. Russia had experienced the world's first successful communist revolution and almost total social breakdown. Huge amounts of money invested in Russia, especially by French investors, were lost. Germany, the world's second largest industrial power, was in chaos for years after the war, a situation made worse by the attempt to recoup the cost of the war through reparations. In 1923, Germany suffered hyperinflation, which made the Deutschmark virtually worthless and destroyed the savings of the middle class. In Britain, long-term unemployment became an unshakeable feature of life in the industrial and mining areas of northern England, Scotland and Wales.

This French newspaper illustration from October 1923 accompanied a report about the effects of hyperinflation in Germany: for example, people in Berlin were looting foodstores.

For a while, in the mid-1920s, it seemed as if 'normalcy' might be restored. In 1925, Britain returned to the gold standard (suspended in 1919), which had provided the sure basis of world trade before the war. In the USA, a consumer boom created the first car-owning society. Even Germany made a frail recovery, based on short-term loans from the USA.

Crash and depression

But in October 1929 prices on the US stock market collapsed. This stock market crash marked the onset of a world-wide economic slump, known as the Great Depression. In 1930, production figures in the USA began to plummet – between 1929 and 1931 production of automobiles halved. In 1931, a bank collapse in Austria set off a chain-reaction of bank failures across Germany. Britain was forced to abandon the gold standard, devaluing its currency. Factories shut

A cartoon about the effect of the Wall Street crash on the stockbroker members of a gentlemen's club.

The Wall Street crash

In the second half of the 1920s, share prices on the USA's Wall Street stock exchange rose rapidly. Dishonest speculators made fortunes and millions of ordinary people were tempted to place their savings in shares.

In the autumn of 1929, however, the stock market bubble burst. In the last week of October, share prices plummeted as panicking investors rushed to sell. Many people suffered financial ruin and confidence in the economy was undermined.

The real-life effect of the crash on one US car-owner.

down and unemployment soared: by 1932, one in five British workers, one in four American workers, and two in five German workers were out of a job.

Instead of cooperating to try to deal with the crisis, countries took the line of 'every man for himself'. They introduced heavy import duties to protect their agriculture and industries from foreign competition. They also devalued their currencies, in an attempt to boost their exports by making their products cheaper for foreigners to buy. But the only result of these policies was to send world trade into a steep downward spiral. By 1932, world trade had fallen by 60 per cent since 1929. Trade was mostly by bilateral agreement, with quotas and deals on prices.

Not unnaturally, some people felt that the economic collapse of the Depression represented the death of capitalism, long predicted by Marxists. It occurred when, for the first time, an alternative way of running a modern economy was being tried out, in the Soviet Union – the product of the Russian Revolution of 1917. Just as the Depression struck, communist dictator Joseph Stalin was launching a

Smoking chimneys

Max Schachtman, an American left-wing radical, looked back on the impression made by the growth of Soviet industry, while the Depression reigned in the USA:

'What stood out in the mind of 99 out of every 100 American radicals was this contrast: there was no smoke in American factory chimneys; there [in Russia] production was going on like mad; everybody was working.'

During the Great Depression, two unemployed men look for work, on foot.

NEXT TIME TRY THE TRAIN
RELAX Southern Pacific

31

"Surpluses and hunger

One of the most powerful arguments against capitalism in the 1930s was the existence of surplus production in industry and agriculture at the same time that many people were hungry and short of clothes and furniture. One person who became disillusioned with capitalism as a result was the famous scientist Albert Einstein (1879-1955). He believed that

'the present economic crisis is due to our system of production for profit rather than for use, to the fact that our tremendous increase of productive power is not actually followed by a corresponding increase in the purchasing power of the great masses.'

Five-Year Plan intended to achieve rapid industrialization in the USSR, under total state control, without either a free market or private capital. To some observers, this appeared to be the way of the future. There was much admiration for the system of state planning, as Soviet industry apparently grew while industry in the capitalist world stagnated. Little was known outside the Soviet Union about the cost of Stalin's policies, including mass famine and the use of political prisoners as slave labour.

Soviet propaganda photographs like this one convinced many people in the West that Soviet agriculture was flourishing. In reality, starvation and terror were the lot of millions of Soviet peasants.

State control

In the 1920s and 1930s, the notion that capitalism went hand in hand with liberal parliamentary government broke down. In Italy, a Fascist dictator, Benito Mussolini, came to power in 1923. He instituted a system known as corporatism, in which employers and workers were supposed to contribute to the common good of the nation under the direction of the state. Mussolini's corporatism, a kind of state-controlled capitalism, found many imitators, especially in Latin America.

In Germany, Adolf Hitler's Nazi Party came to power in January 1933. Under Hitler's dictatorship German capitalism flourished. Strong government restored business confidence, and policies of rearmament and high government spending quickly ended mass unemployment. Capitalists complained about increasing state interference in their business, but it seemed a small price to pay for the crushing of the trade unions and communists.

The New Deal

Even in the USA, the Depression led to an abandonment of pure free-market capitalism and a growth of interference in the economy by the federal government. Franklin D. Roosevelt took office as president in 1933 and dramatically launched his 'New

Cut or spend

The Depression of the early 1930s was viewed by traditional economists as a standard example of part of a healthy business cycle in action. They believed that, since such a cycle brought booms and slumps at intervals, the best remedy for the slump was simply to wait for it to end, which it automatically would. Governments needed only to stand aside, keeping their budgets balanced by cutting spending. This is the policy that Britain and many other countries followed. However, the persistence of the Depression suggested that the classical economists might be wrong. Their opponents, such as John Maynard Keynes (see page 35), said that there was no natural way the slump would end, and that cutting government spending would only make it worse. Governments should increase spending in order to stimulate demand for goods and create employment. This is effectively what the governments of both the USA and Germany did, with some success.

Deal' to get the USA back to work. Roosevelt was in no sense a socialist, but he did represent the perception that capitalism would no longer work if left to itself. The New Deal attempted to make capitalism work by many methods regarded before as alien to capitalism.

This cartoon from 1933 expresses the view that lots of the money Roosevelt's government was borrowing for the New Deal was being wasted – and so the taxpayers kept being asked for more.

To tackle unemployment, Roosevelt's administration set people to work on public projects, paid for with money borrowed by the government – 'deficit spending', as advocated by J. M. Keynes. To tackle low farm prices, the government offered farmers a guaranteed price for their products in return for agreements to cut back production. In industry, business competitors were encouraged to get together to fix prices, stopping competitive price cuts that were forcing everyone to cut wages and lay off workers. The administration also actively encouraged labour unions to fight for better pay and conditions. A start was made on introducing pensions and unemployment benefits, in which the USA lagged far behind most of Europe.

Back to war

Roosevelt's New Deal was immensely popular and he easily won reelection in 1936, but a new recession in 1938 returned US unemployment to high levels.

The Swedish example

From 1920 onwards, government in Sweden was dominated by the Social Democrat party. During the Depression of the 1930s, Swedish economists such as Gunnar Myrdal (1898-1987) persuaded the government to borrow money to pay for jobs. Sweden also introduced an impressive welfare system, with a publicly funded health service, education and social security. The country became a model of the mixture of a free-market economy with elements of socialism. Taxation was high, yet so was economic growth, and a large measure of equality was achieved.

John Maynard Keynes (1883-1946)

English economist J. M. Keynes came to prominence when he attacked the peace treaty at the end of the First World War, claiming that the attempt to take reparation payments from Germany would be impossible and harmful. During the Depression of the 1930s, he argued that there was nothing natural about full employment. He said that mass unemployment could become a permanent state if there was insufficient demand – not enough money chasing goods to buy. He suggested that full employment could be achieved, but only if governments took action to increase demand in the economy. This they would do by running a budget deficit – borrowing money to finance spending. This 'deficit spending' would stimulate the economy and eventually create full employment.

Burying money

Keynes believed that any form of employment was better for the economy than unemployment. He jokingly suggested that, if governments were to

'fill old bottles with banknotes, bury them at suitable depths in disused coalmines which are then filled up to the surface with town rubbish, and leave it to private enterprise ... to dig the notes up again ... there need be no more unemployment and ... the real income of the community ... would probably become a good deal greater than it actually is.'

Keynes's views were attacked by conventional economists, who regarded it as a government's duty to balance its budget, but they were very influential among President Roosevelt's advisers during the New Deal. Keynes was an important figure in working out the Bretton Woods agreements towards the end of the Second World War, and his name is associated with the policies of 'managed' capitalism, designed to produce full employment, widely adopted after 1945.

New Deal policies had failed to solve the long-term problems of capitalism. It was the Second World War that eventually shocked the US economic system out of depression. The USA became a great weapons factory, bringing back full employment and soon forcing up wages as the demand for labour exceeded supply.

During the war, German business corporations were happy to use the slave labour provided by the Nazis – Jews, political prisoners, prisoners of war, and conscript labour from occupied countries. Vast profits were made out of these victims of the Nazis, who were sometimes literally worked to death. It was the most complete demonstration that capitalism and freedom did not necessarily go together.

Planning for the future

In the Allied countries there was a widespread determination that the mass unemployment of the Depression years should not be allowed to return after the war. An international conference held at Bretton Woods, New Hampshire, in 1944 agreed the outlines of a new capitalist world order. Measures were put in place for a gradual resumption of free trade and to stabilize exchange rates against the dollar. Full employment was adopted as an aim of economic policy. The IMF (International Monetary Fund) and the World Bank were established as international organizations designed to intervene in favour of world economic growth and financial stability.

At the end of the Second World War, however, the prospects for a revival of the capitalist system seemed very uncertain. The communist world, dominated by the Soviet Union, was expanding. By 1950, communist governments controlled a huge area from eastern Germany to China. It was an open question whether capitalism or communism would be the economic system of the future.

Capitalism Delivers the Goods

At the end of the Second World War, in 1945, much of the world was in ruins. Among the major powers, only the USA had been enriched by the war. In 1945 it was responsible for two-thirds of the world's entire industrial production. In Germany and Japan, millions of people struggled for mere survival amid the rubble of bomb-flattened cities. Even in Britain, one of the victors, the government was virtually bankrupt and severe shortages of food and fuel continued long after the war ended.

Quite unexpectedly, however, within a few years of the war's end, a period of extraordinary economic growth began in the capitalist world.

This advertisement for a new fridge, from 1950, conveys the excitement created by all the new consumer products in this period.

Between 1950 and 1970, world output of manufactured goods more than quadrupled. Instead of returning to pre-war mass unemployment, by the 1960s Western Europe was experiencing labour

Immigrants from the West Indies arrive in Southampton, UK, 1962.

In Japan, tractors made by the Nissan Automobile Company were ready for export by March 1949.

shortages, sucking in immigrant workers from Southern Europe, Turkey, North Africa, the West Indies and Asia. Industrial wages rose sharply – in Western Europe they doubled in 15 years. This 'economic miracle' was especially striking in West Germany and Japan, which blossomed from war-time devastation into unprecedented productivity. Specializing in growth areas such as electronic goods, Japan had become the world's second largest industrial power by the 1970s.

Much of this boom consisted of Europe and Japan catching up with American technology, and therefore, not surprisingly, it was most effective in the countries that had lost most in the war. Also, the boom was fuelled by turning rural peasants into urban workers, a process that transformed countries such as Italy, France and Spain, as well as Japan.

The economic success story occurred during a period of prolonged international tension as the capitalist 'Free World' confronted the communist Soviet Union and its allies in the Cold War. In fact, the USA's desire to combat communism was one of the main reasons for the economic boom. It made the Americans willing to finance the recovery of their allies, most notably through the Marshall Plan, which from 1948 to 1950 channelled large amounts of US aid into Western Europe. And it led to massive investment by the US government in arms production, which stimulated industrial growth.

Welfare capitalism

The successful capitalism of the post-war period was far removed from the successful capitalism of the pre-1914 period. Most West European countries adopted semi-socialist 'mixed economies', with typically about one-third of industry under state control or state ownership. In Britain, for example, coalmines, railways and steel were among industries nationalized. The idea of economic planning, first tried out in the Soviet Union in the 1930s, was also popular. In France, in particular, a rapid modernization of the economy was achieved under a series of government plans through the 1950s. In Japan, too, the government became heavily involved in the direct promotion of economic growth, in alliance with business corporations.

Keynesian economic policies were widely adopted, with governments increasing spending when necessary to increase demand and maintain full employment. The USA remained in theory committed to balancing the budget and encouraging private entrepreneurs, but the arms race with the Soviet Union drove US government spending inexorably upward.

The new corporation

During this period observers were struck by a fundamental change in the nature of capitalist companies. Traditionally, businesses had been run by the people who owned them. But the huge business corporations of the modern era, such as IBM, General Electric, or ICI, were owned by a wide range of shareholders, from pension funds to small investors, and run by professional managers on a salary. These corporations were generally stable, self-satisfied organizations, which offered lifelong careers and the prospect of a solid pension to the 'corporate men' who worked in their lavish offices. They were very concerned with their public image, and maintained a high quality of product and customer service. They also prided themselves in being generous in their treatment of their workers. Such organizations were far removed from the risk-taking, cut-throat entrepreneurial businesses of an earlier capitalist era.

The rigours of capitalism were mitigated by welfare-state measures which provided a new level of financial security, health care and education for all, or most, citizens. Strong trade unions protected many workers from the power of their employers. In Europe, the need for greater equality in society was widely accepted. Graduated income tax, applied at punitive levels to high incomes, was used in many countries, notably Britain, Sweden and Denmark, as a way of redistributing wealth from the rich to the poor. Money taken from the well-off as taxes was spent on providing worse-off people with welfare payments, free healthcare and education, and cheap homes.

Conservative critics suggested that high taxes and government spending would lead to economic decline, but the facts seemed to prove them wrong. Through the 1950s and 1960s, living standards in the 'developed' world – chiefly North America, Western Europe and Japan – rose at astonishing speed. First in

The affluent society

In 1958, Canadian-born American economist J. K. Galbraith published a book called *The Affluent Society*. Galbraith argued that the ability of capitalism to produce ever greater quantities of goods for people to buy was not creating a happy or well-balanced society. He described the USA in the 1950s as a place of 'private opulence and public squalor', because not enough resources were being devoted to public services such as schools, hospitals or even roads. He also pointed out that pockets of extreme poverty continued to exist in the midst of American affluence. He called for a shift of emphasis from the production of consumer goods to the satisfaction of real human needs.

the USA and then in other developed countries, ownership of cars, fridges, washing machines, telephones and televisions became the norm. In this 'consumer society' advertising was one of the largest growth areas. Young people with money in their pockets paid for the products of a new 'youth culture' of pop music and fashion.

Soviet cosmonaut Yuri Gagarin's journey into space in 1961 made world history – and was seen as a triumph for communism. Here Gagarin and his wife (left) peruse press reports of his achievement, with Soviet leader Nikita Khrushchev and his wife.

Communist challenge

Nonetheless, the communist economies continued to pose a challenge – an apparently viable economic alternative – to capitalism. In 1956, Soviet leader Nikita Khrushchev boasted that communism would 'bury capitalism' through its superior technological and economic performance. It did not, at the time, seem an impossible claim – after all, the Soviet Union was the first country to send a man into space, in 1961.

The communist system was especially attractive to people in the impoverished areas of Africa, Asia and Latin America. Known at the time as the 'Third World', these vast areas of the globe had not tasted the prosperity seen in Europe and North America. They

were at the wrong end of the capitalist system,
exploited as a source of cheap raw materials and a
market for industrial goods, or simply ignored in age-
old poverty, made worse by rapid population growth.

From the 1940s to the 1970s the old European
empires fell apart, and country after country gained
independence. Many of the newly independent
countries of Africa and Asia identified capitalism with
imperialism, the power they had struggled to free
themselves from. Therefore, it seemed essential to them
to resist the capitalist system as part of asserting their
national independence. The power of the capitalist
world economy over Third World countries was
described as 'neo-colonialism'. In the 1960s the idea

Opposing views in India

The largest country to achieve independence from colonial rule in the post-war
period was India. The most famous leader of the Indian independence
movement, Mahatma Gandhi, rejected both capitalism and industry. He saw
India's future as lying in a return to village crafts such as hand-weaving of
textiles. But Jawaharlal Nehru, who led India after independence, favoured
Soviet-style planning and industrialization under state control. These policies
failed to give India the
dynamic economic
growth that Nehru
had hoped for,
however. By the
1990s, India had
accepted the need for
free-market reforms.

**Gandhi at a spinning
wheel, 1931.**

Julius Nyerere (1922-99)

Nyerere was one of the most respected of the first generation of post-colonial African rulers. He became the first president of Tanganyika (later Tanzania) at independence in 1962 and ruled the country for 23 years. He was convinced that capitalism was an alien system that had been wrongly imposed on Africa by European imperialists. In 1967, in the Arusha Declaration, he announced that Tanzania was to embrace an African form of socialism based on rural collectives. Nyerere was an incorruptible individual, who paid himself just £4,000 a year. He earned the enduring love and respect of his people. But his economic policy proved ruinous. By the time he left power, Tanzania was heavily in debt and many of its people were on the edge of starvation.

President Julius Nyerere announces his plan for socialism in Tanzania, in the 'Arusha Declaration', Dar es Salaam, 1967.

emerged of a revolution by the peoples of the Third World, to overthrow capitalism. Communist leaders Mao Tse-tung of China, Ho Chi Minh of Vietnam and Fidel Castro of Cuba were taken as role models by would-be revolutionaries.

Anti-capitalist rebels were not confined to the Third World. In the developed countries, growing prosperity did not create a climate of uncritical acceptance of capitalism. On the contrary, a host of anti-capitalist movements and ideas proliferated, especially among

43

In 1969, 'Life' magazine reported on Hippies who were setting up communes, rejecting consumerist, capitalist values.

young people in the 1960s, in North America and Western Europe. Hippies and others rejected the obsession with consumer goods, work and money, denouncing Western capitalist culture as a spiritual desert. Later, the ecology movement denounced the pollution of the atmosphere and the destruction of the environment in order to satisfy the greed of capitalist enterprises. More traditional Marxists pointed out that poverty and exploitation remained rife amid the prosperity of the consumer boom.

The boom ends

What neither supporters nor critics of the capitalist system at the beginning of the 1970s expected was an end to rapid economic growth in the developed world. But by 1975 the boom had ended, and indeed gone into reverse. Inflation rocketed under the influence of a sharp rise in oil prices (from $3.73 a barrel in 1973 to $33.50 in 1980) and high government spending – at one point in Britain the rate of annual price rises topped 30 per cent. The stable exchange rates which had formed the basis of world trade since the Bretton Woods Conference of 1944 were abandoned in 1971. As economic growth ground to a halt, millions were thrown out of work.

The return of mass unemployment, in places on the same scale as in the 1930s, was a severe shock. It was the result of a number of factors, including increasing automation in factories, replacing workers with machines, and competition from low-paid workers in Third World countries – people employed in clothing factories in Britain, for example, lost their jobs because the same clothes could be made more cheaply in Asia. Whatever the reasons, the comfortable reign of Keynesian economics and welfare capitalism was at an end.

Privatization and Globalization

The recession of the mid-1970s won a new hearing for economists such as Milton Friedman and Friedrich Hayek. They had argued consistently against Keynesian state management of the economy, the welfare state and state control of industries. These economists said that the answer to the new crisis was for governments to abandon involvement in the economy and let the free market and free enterprise do their job of creating wealth. Governments should cut taxes, which discouraged hard work and enterprise, and they should reduce welfare spending to balance their budgets. They should not interfere with wages, prices or investment. Unemployment should be allowed to settle at its 'natural' level, which might be far short of

Milton Friedman (b. 1912)

Milton Friedman of the University of Chicago School was one of the economists who argued for a return to pure capitalism. He advocated 'small government' and regarded attempts to promote equality or social security as misguided. He emphasized that economic growth had always been produced by unfettered entrepreneurs. He advocated monetarism (see page 47). He was awarded the Nobel Prize for Economic Science in 1976, became an economic adviser to US President Ronald Reagan in the early 1980s, and was a leading influence on British Prime Minister Margaret Thatcher.

Friedrich von Hayek (1899-1992)

Austrian-born economist Friedrich von Hayek was one of the most outspoken opponents of socialism and Keynesianism. In his book *The Road to Serfdom*, published in 1944, he argued that only free-market capitalism could allow people to live in a free society. According to Hayek, any form of state control over economic activity was bound to lead to the loss of individual freedom and the abuse of human rights. He was joint winner of the Nobel Prize for Economic Science in 1974.

full employment. One positive role for government was to crack down on the power of trade unions, which were seen as responsible for keeping wages artificially high and thus promoting both inflation and unemployment.

The argument for a return to classic free-market capitalism largely set the agenda for the 1980s and 1990s. It was taken up with most enthusiasm by Margaret Thatcher, British prime minister from 1979 to 1990. The first effect of these policies was to boost unemployment in Britain to levels not seen since the 1930s. Thatcher began a process of 'privatization' – the selling-off of state-controlled industries and utilities – which was later imitated in other European countries, ending the era of the 'mixed economy'.

Supporters of free-market capitalism, UK Prime Minister Margaret Thatcher and US President Ronald Reagan, July 1984.

US President Ronald Reagan was very much in favour of the free market, although he failed to balance his own budget. Under President Bill Clinton from 1994, however, the USA did make progress towards balancing government revenue and expenditure. Cuts in spending included undoing much of what was left of the New Deal welfare

Against government

Ronald Reagan, US president in the 1980s, succinctly rejected the idea that a government had a role in running the economy:

'Government is not the solution but the problem.'

Monetarism

Monetarism was an economic theory that came into fashion in the 1980s.
It focused on the problem of inflation – that is, rising prices. Monetarists
argued that attempts by governments to pump up demand and cut
unemployment only fuelled inflation, because they put too much money in
circulation. Instead, governments should concentrate on keeping the money
supply – the amount of notes and coins in circulation – under control.
Whenever inflation threatened, it was necessary to raise the interest rates
paid by borrowers. This would discourage borrowing – and borrowing was
the chief source of excess money coming into use. Governments must also
avoid borrowing themselves. If governments followed this policy, inflation
would be defeated and the economy would look after itself. Business would
see to it that output increased and unemployment would find its 'natural level'.

system. Japan and countries in mainland Europe were generally more reluctant to dismantle government bureaucracies, or reduce welfare, or open up their countries to full competition.

At the mercy of the markets

But, increasingly, countries had little choice as to what economic policies to follow. By the 1980s, governments had agreed to allow the free movement of capital – that is, people could move large sums of money from one country to another, and from one currency to another, whenever they wished. If financiers, in control of large capital sums, disapproved of a national government's policies, they could quickly shift their money elsewhere. This soon undermined the nation's currency and its economy. This happened to France in the early 1980s. A new president, François Mitterand, was elected and tried to carry through a socialist economic policy, including taking some industries under state control. But the French franc lost value as money was withdrawn from France, and the government was forced to change its policies to ones that the international moneymen approved of.

47

Also, the world's largest companies were no longer confined to a single country. They had become 'multinationals' (or 'transnationals'), operating directly or through subsidiaries in countries across the world. The choices that these multinationals made of where to invest and open new factories gave them enormous power over national economies. If they withdrew their investment and their business, the effect could be devastating.

Employees at a new car assembly plant opened in Indiatuba, Brazil, by the Japanese Toyota Corolla company, September 1998.

The multinationals moved investment around the world partly in pursuit of cheap labour. Workers in the developed countries of Western Europe and North America had become better paid. Also, over the years, their governments had imposed a wide range of regulations on businesses, for example stopping the use of child labour and setting rules to protect workers' health and safety. Multinationals were tempted to open factories in the Third World, where wages were low and working conditions were unregulated, for this cut their costs. Their investment was welcomed by people in relatively impoverished parts of the world for whom poor jobs were better than no jobs at all.

Multinationals also shifted investment between different developed countries. In the 1980s, even the USA had to get used to the experience of some of its major corporations being owned by Japanese capitalists, and its workers being employed in Japanese-owned factories. By the mid–1990s, some 30 Korean companies had factories in Britain. Such investments were dependent on governments pursuing policies that the multinationals considered good for business.

Producing across the world

The German car company Volkswagen shows the trend towards multinational production. By the 1980s, it had factories in Brazil, Canada, Ecuador, Egypt, Mexico, Nigeria, Peru, South Africa and Yugoslavia. National governments could have little control over a company capable of opening or closing factories almost anywhere in the world at will.

Debt and poverty

If major developed nations found it hard to control their own economies, naturally poorer developing nations of Africa, South America and South Asia found it even harder. By the early 1980s, almost without exception, they had fallen heavily into debt, after borrowing to fund industrialization and to pay for food imports, made necessary by the decline of their agriculture. Once in debt, they were at the mercy of the International Monetary Fund (IMF), without whose backing they would have gone bankrupt.

The IMF was totally committed to the new economic orthodoxy and imposed its policies in return for financial support. Country after country was forced to dismantle or slim down its state sector, cut welfare and health spending, and introduce measures to guarantee free competition and encourage private enterprise.

The result was generally encouraging success for some homegrown businesses and small farmers, but intense hardship for much of the poverty-stricken population, whose condition was worsened by failing health care and lost jobs.

By contrast, a small number of 'Third World' countries actually achieved an economic take-off in the 1970s and 1980s. The 'Asian Tigers' – Taiwan, South Korea, Malaysia, Indonesia, Hong Kong and Singapore – achieved outstanding economic growth rates. Taiwan and South Korea virtually joined the club of the developed nations. Their secret appeared to be a hardworking and educated workforce, a skilful business class, and enthusiastic support for business from government.

A shopping mall in Kuala Lumpur, Malaysia – one sign of the economic success of this 'Asian Tiger' country.

The collapse of communism

The most spectacular triumph of capitalism came at the end of the 1980s with the sudden and comprehensive collapse of Soviet communism in Russia and eastern Europe. Hopes that economic growth under communism might match or even outstrip capitalism had proved a delusion. Through the 1970s and 1980s communist economies ran into increasing difficulties, but attempts at a measure of free-market reform and political liberalism in the Soviet Union only created greater instability and economic breakdown. By 1991 the Soviet Union had ceased to exist. Even in China, where the communist party remained in control, the economy was transformed into a form of controlled capitalism. No major alternative to capitalism any longer existed.

The inhabitants of Russia and Eastern Europe were unfortunate that the collapse of communism occurred at a time when the West had become convinced of the virtues of absolute free-market capitalism. Twenty years earlier, there might have been a more gradual transition to the kind of mixed economy and welfare state then prevalent in Western Europe. Instead, state-controlled economies were privatized virtually overnight and welfare provisions that might have cushioned the effect of rapid change were hurriedly abandoned.

Exposed to the cold winds of competition, most parts of Eastern Europe and the former Soviet Union were soon areas of high unemployment, mounting poverty and insecurity. There were small pockets of prosperity, and a small minority of businessmen, many barely legal or frankly outside the law, became extremely rich. But in much of the former communist bloc death rates actually rose in the 1990s, an unprecedented reversal of a long-term trend to longer life.

A homeless child outside a luxury clothing shop in the Bulgarian capital Sofia, November 1997.

In search of free trade

By the 1990s, the whole world was caught up in the drive for 'globalization'. Free trade had been expanded through different rounds of the GATT (General Agreement on Tariffs and Trade) talks. These sought not only to ensure the free movement of goods and capital across frontiers but also to see that governments did not give unfair advantage to their own industries or agriculture – for example, by subsidies. Countries also responded to the increasingly multinational nature of capitalism by creating international free-trade blocs. The European Union and the North American Free Trade Aea were created in 1992 and 1993 respectively. The World Trade Organization (WTO) was founded as a successor to GATT in 1995.

Banana war

The effort to establish absolute free trade and equal competition across national borders through the GATT talks and, since 1995, the World Trade Organization, has been highly controversial. Critics argue that this process has been designed to overcome any resistance to the power of major multinational corporations, for example by outlawing measures to protect small-scale producers in poorer countries. In 1999, for instance, the WTO ruled that the European Union should stop giving favourable treatment to imports of bananas from producers in the West Indies, compared with bananas from American-owned plantations in Latin America. The EU argued that this ruling could ruin West Indian banana growers, crippling the economies of countries that were already poverty-stricken.

A banana grower in Honduras, 1998.

At the Frankfurt stock exchange. Fortunes were made in the 1990s as share prices boomed, especially those of computer and telecommunications companies.

In the later 1990s, the maturing of the computer revolution and the appearance of the Internet produced a new surge in growth rates in developed countries. Companies merged into ever larger units to compete in the global market. Despite much talk of a 'trickledown effect' of wealth from the rich to the poor, however, inequality also tended to increase, both within societies and internationally. The profits and the wealth of entrepreneurs were shamelessly flaunted, as they had been in capitalism's 'golden age'. The triumph of capitalism could hardly have been more complete. Yet strong doubts persisted about the capitalist system, and protests continued against its impact on people's lives across the world.

Challenges for the Future

On 30 November 1999, demonstrators took to the streets of the American city of Seattle, where a summit meeting of the World Trade Organization (WTO) was due to begin. There were clashes with police and a minority of protesters ran riot, smashing the windows of businesses. The demonstrators included many diverse groups, including 'green' environmentalists, trade unionists, animal rights activists and anarchists. But they had all responded to an appeal for what one Internet website called 'a global day of action, resistance and carnival against the global capitalist system'. Obviously, at the end of the second millennium, lots of people were still unhappy about living in a capitalist world.

Protest marchers make their way through the centre of Seattle, 3 December 1999.

Against global capital

Thomas Traviss, a radical journalist wrote about the protests in Seattle in 1999:

'The WTO's program of total liberalization of trade restrictions is only one example of the escalating struggle between the world's rich and the rest of us ... Global capital is trying to remove any and all barriers to its wealth and domination. In this way, the WTO's program is really just the logical extension of an illegitimate system, which places profits before human needs.' (The People's Tribune)

54

Betting on futures

One of the most unstable elements of capitalism at the end of the second millennium was the intense speculation in financial markets and on stock exchanges. For example, the price of shares in new Internet or 'dot.com' companies rose to fabulous heights, despite the fact that many of these companies were doing very little business or making huge losses. When some dot.com companies collapsed in early 2000, there were fears of a possible stock market crash like that of 1929.

Watching a computer monitor at the Hong Kong stock exchange, October 1997, when share prices crashed to record lows.

Global instability

One issue was clearly whether capitalism could, in its own terms, go on delivering the goods – that is, ever-increasing material output. Global capitalism might appear to have triumphed, but it was far from achieving the stability of the pre-1914 period. Exchange rates were liable to extreme fluctuations and stock markets were notoriously unstable. The ease with which massive sums of money could be moved around the globe at the press of a computer key, and the intensity of speculation, created constant fears of a possible crash. In 1997-98, the Pacific Rim economies went into meltdown, with their currencies tumbling and businesses going bankrupt. The area of the former Soviet Union was also a possible source of instability, riven by gangsterism and local wars.

Poverty and the environment

Even if capitalism did function effectively, could it deliver rising living standards for most people? Could it provide for needs such as security and health care, as well as delivering CDs and trainers? Could it lessen inequality and the poverty in which much of the world's population lived? Across the world real incomes more than tripled in the 20th century. But in poorer countries such as India and China, and in much of Africa, average income per head at the end of the century was about one-twentieth of the level in the most developed countries, and the gap was apparently growing. Some people argued that globalization would reverse this trend towards inequality – but as much by reducing the pay of workers in the richer countries as by improving conditions in poorer countries. Many of the protesters in Seattle in 1999 were American workers complaining about the threat to their jobs posed by imports from countries where labour is cheaper.

Banning child labour

The issues that arise in a global capitalist economy are often complex. For example, the governments of the world's richer countries are trying to insist that poorer countries stop the use of child labour. This could be seen as a praise-worthy attempt to prevent multinationals exploiting the world's poorest people for maximum profit – children are always the cheapest workers. But the governments of poorer countries tend to resist the pressure to end child labour. They argue that the rich countries are simply trying to protect the interests of their own pampered, overpaid workforces, at the expense of the poorest people in the world, who could not survive if their children did not work.

Commercialization

By the end of the 20th century, the power of money had spread into every area of life. Sport was a good example. As late as the 1960s, many areas of sport, including the Olympics and Wimbledon tennis, were still amateur. Even professional sports such as football were relatively small-scale business, depending on income from fans paying for low-priced tickets. Nowadays, in all sports, players have become mobile advertising billboards, their shirts and other kit plastered with sponsors' logos. TV companies, owned by multinational

corporations, have pumped huge sums of money into sports, making them big business and ensuring fabulous incomes for star competitors.

German racing driver Michael Schumacher, used as a billboard.

There is also the crucial issue of the impact on the environment, which concerned many of the Seattle protesters. The pursuit of profit has often been destructive both of the natural world and of the local communities that depend on it. The principle of capitalism has always been to pursue a constant and theoretically limitless growth in economic activity. Few people now believe that such growth is sustainable without consequences for the environment which would eventually be economically disastrous, as well as morally wrong. But could capitalism thrive in a world of 'zero growth', as proposed by some ecologists?

In the 1990s world leaders undoubtedly took seriously the need to stop the devastation of the environment by ever-expanding economic activity and the need to tackle the problem of poverty in the developing

Profit or progress

Doubts about the capitalist system are often linked to fears about the impact of technological innovations that are being promoted by multinational companies. For example, there is intense controversy about the rights and wrongs of introducing genetically-modified (GM) crops and foods. Opponents argue that the business corporations developing GM products are risking damage to the environment and to human health in the ruthless pursuit of profit. But supporters of GM technology claim that it is an example of science backed by private investment finding new solutions to the world's problems – in this case, promising food for the rapidly expanding human population of the twenty-first century.

nations. There was notable progress, from agreements to limit emission of 'greenhouse gases' believed responsible for global warming to the cancelling of part of the debts of the poorest countries. But critics described such steps as always too limited and too late.

The greatest strength of the capitalist system might in the end prove to be its flexibility. In principle, capitalists can make money out of environmentally-friendly projects such as solar-panel heating or electric cars as easily as they can out of petrol engines or

Amartya Sen in New York, after being awarded the Nobel Prize for his contributions to welfare economics, 1998.

Amartya Sen (b. 1933)

In 1998 the Nobel Prize for Economics was awarded to the Indian economist Amartya Sen. This award acknowledged a swing in economic thinking away from the pure free-market capitalist ideas of Friedman and Hayek towards 'welfare economics'. Sen's prime concern is with ways of lessening or eradicating poverty and hunger. He accepts that the economic growth produced by capitalist enterprise is important, but argues that it is also essential to distribute wealth more equally.

nuclear power stations. They can make money out of selling leopard skins, or out of developing a synthetic leopard-skin substitute. They can even make profits out of reducing world poverty, since paying workers in developing countries higher wages would make them capable of buying more products.

Humane and prosperous

Capitalism's defenders could point to real triumphs. By the year 2000, most citizens of the developed capitalist countries enjoyed a large measure of freedom, democracy, and a degree of prosperity that earlier generations would have found incredible. Capitalism could claim to have created the most humane and prosperous societies in the history of the world. Even in poorer parts of the world, most people enjoyed longer lives, a better diet and more opportunities than their parents or grandparents had done. Few people disputed that free-market capitalism was the most efficient method of 'wealth creation' yet devised.

One issue for the twenty-first century was the conflict between global capitalism and democracy. Many people felt they had no control over decisions affecting their lives – and the governments they elected had no control either. The only answer to the uncontrolled global power of growing capitalist corporations might be some form of world government. Optimists could hope for a future of 'capitalism with a human face'.

Taming greed

Capitalist society is built on greed. But, as Milton Friedman said in a magazine interview in 1973:

'What kind of society isn't structured on greed? The problem of social organization is how to set up an arrangement under which greed will do the least harm; capitalism is that kind of system.'

Date List

1771 Richard Arkwright builds a cotton-spinning mill (factory) in Derbyshire, England, one of the first steps in the 'industrial revolution'.

1776 Publication of Adam Smith's *An Inquiry into the Nature and Causes of the Wealth of Nations*, describing how a free-market capitalist system could work.

1811 'Luddites', poor hand-weavers opposed to the introduction of cotton-weaving machinery in the north of England, attack factories and destroy machines.

1817 Publication of David Ricardo's *Principles of Political Economy and Taxation*.

1825 In England, the first public railway is built, between Stockton and Darlington.

1833 The first of the Factory Acts is passed by the British parliament, to improve conditions for factory workers.

1839 Britain launches the first Opium War against China, to force the Chinese to open their ports to foreign trade.

1846 The repeal of the Corn Laws, which imposed a duty on imported wheat, marks the victory of free trade in Britain.

1853 A fleet led by US officer Commodore Perry sails to Japan to force the Japanese to open up their country to Western trade and influence.

1865 In the American Civil War, the industrialized capitalist North defeats the slave-owning South.

1867 Karl Marx publishes the first volume of *Das Kapital*, an immensely influential analysis of, and attack on, capitalism.

1868 Japan begins the move towards Western-style industrial and technological development in the 'Meiji Restoration'.

1871 Germany, formerly a group of separate states of varying sizes, is unified under the leadership of Prussia; Germany soon becomes the world's second greatest industrial power, after the USA.

1890 Anti-trust legislation, the Sherman Act, is passed in the USA. Intended to ensure competition in a free market and prevent companies cooperating to fix prices, it was in practice mostly used against labour unions.

1908 In the USA, Henry Ford introduces the Model T Ford, which will become the first mass-produced automobile.

1914 Start of First World War.

1917 The Russian Revolution establishes the world's first long-lived anti-capitalist government.

1918 First World War ends with Germany in chaos and Britain heavily in debt to the USA.

1923 Hyperinflation destroys the value of the German currency, the Deutschmark.

1925 Dictator Benito Mussolini begins to introduce his new economic system, 'corporatism'.

1929 A stock market crash on Wall Street marks the beginning of the Great Depression.

1932	Unemployment reaches unprecedented levels, especially in the USA and Germany.
1933	Franklin D. Roosevelt takes over as US president and introduces the New Deal. Adolf Hitler takes power in Germany.
1936	John Maynard Keynes publishes his *General Theory of Employment, Interest and Money*.
1939	Start of Second World War.
1940	The US economy begins to grow rapidly as war production gets under way.
1944	The Bretton Woods conference produces a blueprint for the post-war world economy.
1945	A Labour government is elected in Britain, committed to nationalizing major industries and creating a welfare state.
1947	Under the Marshall Plan, the USA provides finance for the rebuilding of the Western European economy.
1949	The Communists take power in China; an alternative system to capitalism now prevails from the Pacific Ocean to central Europe.
1957	The European Economic Community, or Common Market, is founded by the Treaty of Rome.
1969	After two decades of rapid growth, statistics show that Japan has become the world's second largest economy.
1971	The system of fixed currency exchange rates adopted at Bretton Woods is abandoned, as the US economy is hit by inflation and high government spending.

1973	Arab oil producers cut output; as a result, fuel prices in industrialized countries begin to rise rapidly, triggering inflation and mass unemployment.
1974	Friedrich Hayek is awarded the Nobel Prize for Economic Science.
1976	Milton Friedman is awarded the Nobel Prize for Economic Science.
1979	Margaret Thatcher is elected British prime minister; her policy of privatizing nationalized industries will eventually be imitated across Europe.
1980	Ronald Reagan wins US presidential election; he adopts Friedman as an economic adviser.
1989	The fall of the Berlin Wall marks the collapse of communist government across eastern Europe.
1991	The Soviet Union ceases to exist.
1992	The European Union is formed with the aim of eventually creating a single European currency and economy.
1993	The USA, Canada and Mexico form the North American Free Trade Area.
1995	The World Trade Organization is founded.
1997	The rapidly growing economies of South Korea, Taiwan, Singapore, Malaysia and Indonesia are suddenly hit by a severe financial crisis.
1998	Amartya Sen is awarded the Nobel Prize for Economic Science.
1999	Anti-capitalist riots rock Seattle during a meeting of the WTO.

Glossary

cartel
a group of companies that make an agreement to fix prices instead of competing with one another, thus keeping prices, and their profits, high. Another word for a cartel is a 'trust'.

corporatism
economic system in which business remains in private ownership but the state intervenes to make employers and workers cooperate in serving the national interest.

deficit spending
an economic policy in which a government deliberately spends more than its income from taxes, covering the resulting deficit by borrowing. The policy is intended to boost the economy, especially reducing unemployment.

depression
a prolonged period when the economy is in poor shape, marked by high unemployment, the closure of businesses, and widespread poverty.

deregulation
the lifting of government controls on business and finance.

economic planning
an attempt by a government to direct the development of its national economy by setting targets for growth in different sectors and allocating resources to make those targets achievable.

GATT
the General Agreement on Tariffs and Trade, an international agreement to encourage free trade, signed in 1947. In 1995, GATT was superseded by the WTO.

IMF (International Monetary Fund)
a financial organization set up in 1945 to stabilize world trade and lend money to countries that need it. The IMF often insists that countries adopt certain economic policies as a condition of being given a loan.

import duties
taxes imposed by a government on goods imported into their country from abroad. Such duties can be used to make imported goods more expensive, so encouraging people to buy products made in their own country instead.

inflation
a general rise in prices. 'Hyperinflation' is a very rapid accelerating rise in prices.

recession
a temporary decline in the economy, marked by rising unemployment and falling output of goods and services. A recession is less serious than a depression or slump.

socialism
an alternative form of economic organization to capitalism, in which the state owns all, or a large part, of business, industry and land. The economy is directed by the state for the general good of the community, rather than left to the free market; and extremes of individual wealth and poverty are eradicated.

speculation
investing money riskily, in the hope of a profit.

susbsidy
money paid by a government to manufacturers or farmers, to help their business.

tariff
an import duty (see above).

trust – see **cartel**

welfare state
a country in which the state attempts to look after its citizens 'from the cradle to the grave', providing free health care, old age pensions, and benefits for the poor and unemployed.

WTO (World Trade Organization)
an international body set up in 1995 to promote free and fair trade worldwide.

Resources

Reference

The Wealth and Poverty of Nations (1998) by David Landes is a lively and thoughtful book trying to explain why, in the capitalist era, some countries have become poor while others have grown rich.

The Affluent Society (revised edition 1969) by John Kenneth Galbraith is one of the most readable books written by an economist. It includes a good short history of what other economists have thought about capitalism.

Capitalism and Freedom (revised edition 1982) by Milton Friedman is a clear statement of the argument for classic free-market capitalism.

The Road to Serfdom (most recent edition 1994) by Friedrich Hayek is an influential book on the link between freedom and capitalism.

Historian Eric Hobsbawm has written four excellent books covering the period from the 1780s to the 1990s: *The Age of Revolution* (1962), *The Age of Capital* (1975), *The Age of Empire* (1987) and *The Age of Extremes* (1994).

The Communist Manifesto (1848) by Karl Marx is one of the first and most famous attacks on capitalism. It gives a vivid impression of how revolutionary the capitalist system seemed to people in the nineteenth century.

Fiction and humour

A significant percentage of novels and plays written since 1800 include more or less explicit criticism of capitalist society. Few fiction writers have had a good word to say for capitalism!

Charles Dickens' novel *Hard Times* comments directly on early industrialization and the attitudes that went with it. Almost all of Dickens' novels are concerned to some degree with the new type of society capitalism brought to Britain in the nineteenth century.

D. H. Lawrence's novels are packed with hostile comments on the impact of industrial capitalism.

John Steinbeck's *The Grapes of Wrath* is a famous novel about the Depression of the 1930s.

British comic writer Ben Elton has written novels and plays parodying the impact of heartless capitalism on ordinary people and on the environment. In contrast, *Eat the Rich* (1998) by P. J. O'Rourke is an aggressive attack on socialism and defence of capitalism by a right-wing American humourist.

Internet

The League of Revolutionaries for a New America provides a stream of propaganda and debate from an anti-capitalist standpoint at www.lrna.org

Index